QUOTES

Om **Books International**

Reprinted in 2023

Om Books International

Corporate & Editorial Office

A-12, Sector 64, Noida 201 301
Uttar Pradesh, India
Phone: +91 120 477 4100
Email: editorial@ombooks.com
Website: www.ombooksinternational.com

Sales Office

107, Ansari Road, Darya Ganj,
New Delhi 110 002, India
Phone: +91 11 4000 9000
Email: sales@ombooks.com
Website: www.ombooks.com

ISBN: 978-93-85609-94-7

Printed in India

10 9 8 7 6 5 4 3

INTRODUCTION

Some of the finest beacons during life's crests and troughs, have been the writers, philosophers, artists, leaders we have grown up admiring. Be it Rabindranath Tagore or Munshi Premchand's portrayal of human nature, Socrates or Aristotle's philosophical musings, Mahatma Gandhi or Nelson Mandela's fight for freedom, Fyodor Dostoevsky or Alexandre Dumas' analyses of our own multiplicity, Khaled Hosseini or Margaret Atwood's battle with the self— the wisdom of their words continues to nurture the soul.

This collection of inspirational quotes is the perfect companion in life's most trying moments as also when the mind, body and soul are in harmony with each other.

'Darkness cannot drive out darkness: only light can do that. Hate cannot drive out hate: only love can do that.

Martin Luther King

Love all,

trust a few,

do wrong to none.

William Shakespeare

If one wants to be loved,

one must first know

how to love.

Kabir

Courage is grace

under pressure.

Ernest Hemingway

Being deeply loved
by someone gives
you strength, while
loving someone
deeply gives you
courage.

Lao Tzu

For what it's worth,

it's never too late

to be whoever

you want to be.

F. Scott Fitzgerald

Somewhere inside all

of us is the power to

change the world.

Roald Dahl

When things are

really dismal,

you can laugh,

or

you can cave in

completely.

Margaret Atwood

It isn't what we say

or think that

defines us, but

what we do.

Jane Austen

It is courage,

not luck that

takes us through

to the end of

the road.

Ruskin Bond

Wisdom is

often times nearer

when we stoop

than when

we soar.

William Wordsworth

Freedom lies

in being bold.

Robert Frost

Life is really
simple, but we
insist on making it
complicated.

Confucius

Forgiveness is the
fragrance that the violet
sheds on the heel
that has crushed it.

Mark Twain

Intelligence is

the ability to

adapt to change.

Stephen Hawking

Where the
willingness is great,
the difficulties
cannot be great.

Machiavelli

We have

forty million reasons

for failure, but

not a single excuse.

Rudyard Kipling

'

Love recognises

no barriers.

It jumps hurdles,

leaps fences,

penetrates walls to

arrive at

its destination

full of hope.

Maya Angelou

Love does not

claim possession,

but gives freedom.

Rabindranath Tagore

The two

most powerful

warriors are

patience and time.

Leo Tolstoy

There is only

one corner of

the universe

you can be

certain of improving,

and

that's your own self.

Aldous Huxley

Happiness is

when what you think,

what you say,

and

what you do

are in harmony.

Mahatma Gandhi

In the end, it's not the years in your life that count. It's the life in your years.

Abraham Lincoln

We

do not remember

days,

we remember

moments.

Cesare Pavese

We live in a

wonderful world

that is full of beauty,

charm and adventure.

There is no end to the

adventures that

we can have

if only we seek them

with our eyes open.

Jawaharlal Nehru

Mistakes are

the portals of

discovery.

James Joyce

Each person must live their life as a model for others.

Rosa Parks

Peace begins with
a smile.

Mother Teresa

Procrastination is
the thief of time;
collar him.

Charles Dickens

Ours

is an excessively

conscious age.

We know so much,

we feel so little.

D.H. Lawrence

Our deeds
determine us, as
much as
we determine
our deeds.

George Eliot

' Only put off
until tomorrow
what you are
willing to die
having left
undone.

Pablo Picasso

It is never too late

to be what you

might have been.

George Eliot

Joy is the simplest form of

gratitude.

Karl Barth

The mind

is furnished

with ideas by

experience alone.

John Locke

Life isn't about

finding yourself.

Life is about

creating yourself.

George Bernard Shaw

Very little is needed

to make

a happy life;

it is all within yourself,

in your way of thinking.

Marcus Aurelius

You are never

too old to set

another goal

or to dream

a new dream.

C.S. Lewis

Our prime purpose

in this life is

to help others.

And if you can't

help them,

at least don't hurt them.

Dalai Lama

Any man

who stands for progress

has to criticise, disbelieve

and challenge every

item of the old faith.

Bhagat Singh

Better remain silent,

better not even think,

if you are not

prepared to act.

Annie Besant

A man without ethics

is a wild beast

loosed upon this world.

Albert Camus

Who sows virtue

reaps honour.

Leonardo da Vinci

Between the fear

that something would

happen and the hope

that still it wouldn't,

there is much more

space than one thinks.

Ivo Andri□

By failing to

prepare, you are

preparing

to fail.

Benjamin Franklin

Setting goals

is the first step in

turning the invisible

into the visible.

Tony Robbins

Forgiveness is the key to

action and freedom.

Hannah Arendt

Blessed are the hearts
that can bend; they
shall never be broken.

Albert Camus

Bewitched is half

of everything.

Nelly Sachs

The harder

the conflict,

the more glorious

the triumph.

Thomas Paine

The key is to keep company only with people who uplift you, whose presence calls forth your best.

Epictetus

It is very important

to know who you are.

To make decisions.

To show who you are.

Malala Yousafzai

Faith must be breathed to be understood.

Patrick White

Fate is the endless chain of causation, whereby things are; the reason or formula by which the world goes on.

Zeno of Citium

But from each

crime are born

bullets that will

one day seek out

in you where the

heart lies.

Pablo Neruda

Your time is limited,
so don't waste it
living someone
else's life.

Steve Jobs

When something
is important enough,
you do it even if the
odds are not in
your favour.

Elon Musk

Reason

has always existed,

but

not always in a

reasonable form.

Karl Marx

Men would live

exceedingly quiet

if these two words,

mine and thine,

were taken away.

Anaxagoras

Better be wise

by the misfortunes

of others

than by your own.

Aesop

It is love, not reason, that is stronger than death.

Thomas Mann

Let no one be
willing to speak ill
of the absent.

Sextus Propertius

Cultivation of mind

should be

the ultimate aim of

human existence.

B.R. Ambedkar

Knowledge is in
the end based on
acknowledgement.

Ludwig Wittgenstein

To one

who has faith,

no explanation

is necessary.

To one without faith,

no explanation

is possible.

Thomas Aquinas

Nothing great
in the world
has ever been
accomplished
without passion.

Georg Wilhelm Friedrich Hegel

A propensity to hope

and joy is real riches;

one to fear and sorrow,

real poverty.

David Hume

Understanding

is nothing else

than conception

caused by

speech.

Thomas Hobbes

All good things
which exist are the
fruits of originality.

John Stuart Mill

To conquer fear

is the beginning

of wisdom.

Bertrand Russell

One should not be

happy or distressed

over desirables and

undesirables, knowing

that such feelings are

just created by the mind.

A.C. Bhaktivedanta
Swami Prabhupada

Science is

organised

knowledge.

Wisdom is

organised life.

Immanuel Kant

Hope is patience

with the lamp lit.

Tertullian

Hope raises no dust.

Paul Eluard

Intelligence

without ambition is

a bird

without wings.

Salvador Dali

There is nothing

permanent,

except change.

Heraclitus

Gratitude is not only the greatest of virtues, but the parent of all the others.

Marcus Tullius Cicero

Love hard

when there is love

to be had.

Bob Marley

Yesterday is not ours

to recover, but

tomorrow is ours to

win or lose.

Lyndon B. Johnson

Don't grieve.

Anything you lose

comes round

in another form.

Rumi

Ignorance leads to fear,

fear leads to hate, and

hate leads to violence.

This is the equation.

Averroes

To succeed,

you need to

find something

to hold on to,

something

to motivate you,

something

to inspire you.

Tony Dorsett

Your smile will give you

a positive countenance

that will make people

feel comfortable

around you.

Les Brown

If you are

not making mistakes,

then you're

not doing anything.

I am positive that

a doer makes mistakes.

John Wooden

Expectations are

a form of first-class truth:

If people believe it,

it's true.

Bill Gates

Do not dwell in the past,

do not dream

of the future,

and concentrate

the mind on the

present moment.

Gautama Buddha

Better a little
which is well done,
than a great deal
imperfectly.

Plato

Truth is

ever to be found in

simplicity, and not

in the multiplicity and

confusion of things.

Isaac Newton

How very little
can be done under the
spirit of fear.

Florence Nightingale

Great fear is
concealed under
daring.

Lucan

Happiness is your nature.

It is not wrong to desire it.

What is wrong

is seeking it outside

when it is inside.

Sri Ramana Maharshi

Definiteness of purpose

is the starting point of

all achievement.

W. Clement Stone

Life isn't about
getting and having, it's
about giving and being.

Kevin Kruse

Life is 10% what happens
to me and 90% how
I react to it.

Charles R. Swindoll

'The most common way

people give up

their power is

by thinking

they don't have any.

Alice Walker

The true adventurer

goes forth aimless and

uncalculating

to meet and greet

unknown fate.

O. Henry

It is not living that
matters, but
living rightly.

Socrates

It is good to love

many things, for therein

lies the true strength, and

whosoever loves much

performs much, and

can accomplish much,

and what is done in love

is well done.

Vincent van Gogh

Believe in your dream

and that anything

is possible.

Usain Bolt

Few things are impossible

to diligence and skill.

Great works are

performed

not by strength,

but perseverance.

Samuel Johnson

We are what
we repeatedly do.
Excellence, then,
is not an act,
but a habit.

Aristotle

The key is

not the will to win.

Everybody has that.

It is the will

to prepare to win

that is important.

Bobby Knight

Whatever the
mind of man
can conceive and
believe,
it can achieve.

Napoleon Hill

Sometimes we stare

so long at a door

that is closing,

that we see too late

the one that is open.

Alexander Graham Bell

Imagination

rules the world.

Napoleon Bonaparte

True intelligence requires

fabulous imagination.

Ian McEwan

Vision without

execution

is delusion.

Thomas Edison

An obstacle
is often a
stepping stone.

William Prescott

Never give up.

Winston Churchill

It always seems

impossible

until it's done.

Nelson Mandela

God is

not present in idols.

Your feelings are

your god.

The soul is your temple.

Chanakya

Surround yourself

with only people

who

are going to

lift you higher.

Oprah Winfrey

It is not in the stars

to hold our destiny

but in ourselves.

William Shakespeare

There is no

education

like adversity.

Benjamin Disraeli

Put your heart,

mind, and soul

into even your

smallest acts.

This is the secret

of success.

Swami Sivananda

As long as

space abides

and as long as

the world abides,

so long may I abide,

destroying the sufferings

of the world.

Shantideva

The secret of

happiness is

freedom.

The secret of

freedom is

courage.

Thucydides

A calm mind releases
the most precious
capacity a human being
can have: the capacity
to turn anger into
compassion, fear into
fearlessness, and hatred
into love.

Eknath Easwaran

Moderation

in all things.

Publius Terentius Afer

Put more trust

in nobility

of character

than in an oath.

Solon

'

The best way

to keep good acts

in memory is

to refresh them

with new.

Marcus Porcius Cato

Force has no
place where there
is need of skill.

Herodotus

Don't put the key
to your happiness
in someone else's
pocket.

Swami Chinmayananda

By suspending judgment,
by confining oneself to
phenomena or objects
as they appear, and by
asserting nothing definite
as to how they really are,
one can escape the
perplexities of life and
attain an imperturbable
peace of mind.

Pyrrho

Except our own thoughts,

there is nothing absolutely

in our power.

Rene Descartes

Like a flowing river,

what has gone

will never come

back.

Valmiki

Patience is bitter,

but its fruit is sweet.

Jean-Jacques Rousseau

That

which does not kill us

makes us stronger.

Friedrich Nietzsche

Knowledge is power.

Francis Bacon

Freedom is what you do with what's been done to you.

Jean-Paul Sartre

Use your gifts faithfully,
and they shall be
enlarged; practise what
you know, and you
shall attain to higher
knowledge.

Matthew Arnold

Nothing has ever

molded our conscience

so strongly as our

knowledge of what is

good and what is evil.

Bjørnstjerne Bjørnson

Patience is the

companion of

wisdom.

Saint Augustine

True virtue is life under
the direction of reason.

Baruch Spinoza

Virtue is more to be feared
than vice, because its
excesses are not subject
to the regulation of
conscience.

Adam Smith

Appreciation is

a wonderful thing:

It makes what is excellent

in others

belong to us as well.

Voltaire

Change your life today.

Don't gamble

on the future,

act now,

without delay.

Simone de Beauvoir

'

Man's greatness

lies in his power of

thought.

Blaise Pascal

Where there is power, there is resistance.

Michel Foucault

'A man who dares
to waste one hour
of time has not
discovered the
value of life.

Charles Darwin

Education is not

preparation for life;

education is

life itself.

John Dewey

The mind cannot foresee its own advance.

Friedrich August von Hayek

Truth is born

into this world

only with pangs and

tribulations,

and every fresh truth

is received unwillingly.

Alfred Russel Wallace

Change your
thoughts
and you change
your world.

Norman Vincent Peale

Discipline is

the bridge

between goals and

accomplishment.

Jim Rohn

'You must learn

to be still

in the midst of activity, and

to be vibrantly alive

in repose.

Indira Gandhi

When the fight begins

within himself,

a man's worth something.

Robert Browning

To put a
tempting face aside
when duty demands
every faculty,
is a lesson
which takes most men
longest to learn.

Gertrude Atherton

Lack of discipline

leads to frustration

and self-loathing.

Marie Chapian

You must have

discipline

to have fun.

Julia Child

Self-command is

the main elegance.

Ralph Waldo Emerson

Temptations come,

as a general rule,

when they are sought.

Margaret Oliphant

A mind which really lays

hold of a subject is not

easily detached from it.

Ida Tarbell

Too often

in ironing out

trouble

someone gets

scorched.

Marcelene Cox

Bondage and

liberation are

of the mind alone.

Ramakrishna Paramahamsa

When you borrow
trouble, you give
your peace of
mind as security.

Myrtle Reed

Love is that condition

in which

the happiness of

another person

is essential to your own.

Robert A. Heinlein

The most
important thing
when ill, is
to never lose
heart.

Vladimir Lenin

To live a creative life,

we must first lose

the fear of

being wrong.

Joseph Chilton Pearce

'If you desire ease,

forsake learning.

If you desire

learning,

forsake ease.

Nagarjuna

Keep on beginning and failing. Each time you fail, start all over again, and you will grow stronger until you have accomplished a purpose — not the one you began with perhaps, but one you'll be glad to remember.

Anne Sullivan Macy

Life is what

happens to you

while you're busy

making other plans.

John Lennon

In a conflict

between the heart

and the brain,

follow your heart.

Swami Vivekananda

You get ideas from daydreaming. You get ideas from being bored. You get ideas all the time. The only difference between writers and other people is we notice when we're doing it.

Neil Gaiman

Let all listen, and

be willing to listen

to the doctrines

professed by others.

Ashoka

When the mind is
still, then truth gets
her chance to
be heard in the
purity of the silence.

Sri Aurobindo

We become what

we think about.

Earl Nightingale

Laziness may appear attractive, but work gives satisfaction.

Anne Frank

Wisdom

ceases to be wisdom

when it becomes

too proud to weep,

too grave to laugh, and

too selfish to seek other

than itself.

Kahlil Gibran

An art,

which has an aim

to achieve

the beauty,

is called a philosophy

or in the absolute

sense, it is named

wisdom.

Al-Farabi

What you do today

can improve

all your tomorrows.

Ralph Marston

A creative man is motivated by the desire to achieve, not by the desire to beat others.

Ayn Rand

Beauty is mysterious

as well as terrible.

God and devil

are fighting there,

and the battlefield is

the heart of man.

Fyodor Dostoyevsky

Everyone thinks of changing the world, but no one thinks of changing himself.

Leo Tolstoy

For to be free

is not merely

to cast off one's chains,

but to live in a way that

respects and enhances

the freedom of others.

Nelson Mandela

It is by acts

and not by ideas

that people live.

Anatole France

The whole problem
with the world is that
fools and fanatics
are always so certain
of themselves, and
wiser people
so full of doubts.

Bertrand Russell

Don't bother

just to be better than

your contemporaries

or predecessors.

Try to be better than

yourself.

William Faulkner

Let us be grateful

to people who

make us happy,

they are the

charming gardeners who

make our souls blossom.

Marcel Proust

Be on the alert

to recognise your prime

at whatever time

of your life it may occur.

Muriel Spark

We live in a

fantasy world,

a world of illusion.

The great task in life is to

find reality.

Iris Murdoch

If misery loves

company,

then triumph

demands an

audience.

Brian Moore

Self criticism must be
my guide to action,
and the first rule for its
employment is that
in itself it is not a virtue,
only a procedure.

Kingsley Amis

The capacity

you're thinking of is

imagination;

without it

there can be no

understanding.

William Trevor

To love someone

is to see a miracle

invisible to others.

François Mauriac

All great enterprises

are about logistics.

Not genius or

inspiration or

flights of imagination,

skill or cunning,

but logistics.

Tom McCarthy

People always call it luck

when you've acted

more sensibly than

they have.

Anne Tyler

Inspiration comes from
everything
from the entire world,
and it's hard to pinpoint
one thing.

Ruth Ozeki

Inspiration comes of
working every day.

Charles Baudelaire

Happiness

always looks small

while you hold it

in your hands,

but let it go, and

you learn at once

how big and precious

it is.

Maxim Gorky

Be kind, be decent,
be generous, be tolerant,
compassionate, and
understanding. Be fast
to praise, slow to judge.
Remember, we're all
human, and don't cast
the first stone.

Allen Drury

Fear created

the first gods in the world.

Caecilius Statius

God did not intend

religion to be an

exercise club.

Naguib Mahfouz

The facts of life are very
stubborn things.

Cleveland Amory

If you spend your
whole life waiting for
the storm,
you'll never enjoy the
sunshine.

Morris West

To be one's self,

and unafraid whether

right or wrong,

is more admirable than

the easy cowardice of

surrender to conformity.

Irving Wallace

The most beautiful

thing in the world is,

of course,

the world itself.

Wallace Stevens

Good habits

are worth being

fanatical about.

John Irving

Never let your

sense of morals

get in the way of

doing what's right.

Isaac Asimov

Let each man

pass his days in that

wherein his skill

is greatest.

Sextus Propertius

You will become

as small as

your controlling desire;

as great as your

dominant aspiration.

James Allen

Repetition for no reason

is a sign of carelessness

or pretentiousness.

Steven Millhauser

What is sanity, after
all, except the control
of madness?

Josephine Winslow Johnson

The greatest wealth is
to live content with little,
for there is never want
where the mind is
satisfied.

Lucretius

People find meaning

and redemption

in the most unusual

human connections.

Khaled Hosseini

If fortune favours you,

do not be elated;

if she frowns,

do not despond.

Ausonius

The happiness of
your life depends
upon the quality of
your thoughts.

Marcus Aurelius

Happy is the man who

has broken the chains

which hurt the mind, and

has given up worrying

once and for all.

Ovid

Rare is the union of
beauty and purity.

Juvenal

Truth isn't always beauty,
but the hunger for it is.

Nadine Gordimer

No single man can be

taken as a model for a

perfect figure,

for no man lives on Earth

who is endowed with the

whole of beauty.

Albrecht Durer

Everyone ought to
bear patiently the
results of his own
conduct.

Phaedrus

It's no use growing older

if you only learn

new ways of

misbehaving yourself.

Hector Hugh Munro

Changing your mind is probably one of the most beautiful things people can do. And I've changed my mind about a lot of things over the years.

Paul Auster

What a delightful thing

perspective is!

Paolo Uccello

Even if the hopes

you started out with

are dashed, hope

has to be maintained.

Seamus Heaney

Any knowledge that
doesn't lead to
new questions
quickly dies out:
it fails to maintain the
temperature required for
sustaining life.

Wislawa Szymborska

Deserve

your

dream.

Octavio Paz

We make too much of

that long groan which

underlines the past.

Derek Walcott

There are two kinds of
men: the ones
who make history and
the ones who
endure it.

Camilo José Cela

How delightful to find

a friend in everyone.

Joseph Brodsky

The greatest threat to

freedom is

the absence of

criticism.

Wole Soyinka

The voice of passion is

better than

the voice of reason.

The passionless

cannot change

history.

Czeslaw Milosz

Success listens
only to applause. To all
else it is deaf.

Elias Canetti

Success is a science; if
you have the conditions,
you get the result.

Oscar Wilde

The journey of life is like
a man riding a bicycle.

William Golding

One doesn't recognise
the really important
moments in one's life
until it's too late.

Agatha Christie

A man is only
as good as
what he loves.

Saul Bellow

Too many lives

are needed to

make just one.

Eugenio Montale

And this we should believe: that hope and volition can bring us closer to our ultimate goal: justice for all, injustice for no-one.

Eyvind Johnson

Look deep

into nature,

and then

you will understand

everything better.

Albert Einstein

He whose wisdom

cannot help him,

gets no good from

being wise.

Quintus Ennius

It is courage, courage,

courage, that raises

the blood of life to

crimson splendour.

Live bravely and present

a brave front

to adversity.

Horace

You may have heard
the world is made up of
atoms and molecules,
but it's really made up of
stories.

William Turner

Genius is the
ability to renew
one's emotions in
daily experience.

Paul Cezanne

Concentrate your

strengths against

your competitor's

relative weaknesses.

Paul Gauguin

Nature is not only all

that is visible to the eye,

it also includes

the inner pictures

of the soul.

Edvard Munch

Art is not what

you see, but

what you make

others see.

Edgar Degas

They always say
time changes things, but
you actually have to
change them yourself.

Andy Warhol

Time changes everything
except something
within us which is always
surprised by change.

Thomas Hardy

'I never saw an ugly thing in my life: for let the form of an object be what it may—light, shade, and perspective will always make it beautiful.

John Constable

Believe you can and you're halfway there.

Theodore Roosevelt

When you reach

the end

of your rope,

tie a knot in it and

hang on.

Franklin D. Roosevelt

Your success and
happiness lie in you.
Resolve to keep happy,
and your joy and you
shall form an invincible
host against difficulties.

Helen Keller

Things do not happen. Things are made to happen.

John F. Kennedy

Not to unlearn what
you have learned
is the most necessary
kind of learning.

Antisthenes

Hope is the only good
that is common to
all men; those who have
nothing else possess
hope still.

Thales

This is love:

the flowering of love is

meditation.

Jiddu Krishnamurti

We can't command

our love, but we can

our actions.

Arthur Conan Doyle

Love is the only wealth
that man absolutely
needs. Love is the only
wealth that
God precisely is.

Sri Chinmoy

Our own

self-realisation is the

greatest service we

can render the world.

Ramana Maharshi

Say not always

what you know, but

always know what

you say.

Claudius

Yesterday is

but today's memory,

and tomorrow is

today's dream.

Kahlil Gibran

The bad man desires arbitrary power. What moves the evil man is the love of injustice.

John Rawls

What we do upon

some great occasion

will probably depend on

what we already are;

and what we are will

be the result of previous

years of self-discipline.

H.P. Liddon

Knowledge, if it does
not determine action, is
dead to us.

Plotinus

Only divine love bestows
the keys of knowledge.

Arthur Rimbaud

They say

a little knowledge is

a dangerous thing,

but it's not one half

so bad as a lot of

ignorance.

Terry Pratchett

One good turn

deserves another.

Gaius Petronius Arbiter

Courage is of
no value unless
accompanied by
justice; yet if all men
became just, there
would be no need for
courage.

Agesilaus II

How we remember,

what we remember,

and why we

remember

form the most

personal map of our

individuality.

Christina Baldwin

Nothing can be

created from nothing.

Lucretius

Familiarity breeds contempt, while rarity wins admiration.

Apuleius

Many receive advice,

only the wise

profit from it.

Harper Lee

Truth is the cry of all, but the game of few.

George Berkeley

A deception that elevates us is dearer than a host of low truths.

Marina Tsvetaeva

Light is meaningful
only in relation to darkness,
and truth presupposes
error. It is these mingled
opposites which people our
life, which make it pungent,
intoxicating. We only exist
in terms of this conflict,
in the zone where
black and white clash.

Louis Aragon

'Promise me
you'll always
remember:
You're braver than
you believe,
stronger than you
seem, and smarter
than you think.

A.A. Milne

Will cannot be

quenched against

its will.

Dante Alighieri

Forever

is composed of

nows.

Emily Dickinson

Any human anywhere
will blossom in a
hundred unexpected
talents and capacities
simply by being given
the opportunity
to do so.

Doris Lessing

'There are two worlds
we live in:
a material world,
bound by the laws of
physics, and the world
inside our mind, which
is just as important.

Alan Moore

If you lose sight of the smaller accomplishments, you end up with an imbalance in your life.

Alexander McCall Smith

All human wisdom is

contained in

these two words:

wait and hope.

Alexandre Dumas

The true genius
shudders at
incompleteness —
and usually prefers
silence to saying
something which
is not everything it
should be.

Edgar Allan Poe

Evil is whatever

distracts.

Franz Kafka

To me an unnecessary action, or shot, or casualty, was not only waste but sin.

T.E. Lawrence

What matters in life

is not what happens

to you but what you

remember and how

you remember it.

Gabriel Garcia Marquez

Without a struggle,

there can be no progress.

Frederick Douglass

Among the many values
in life, I appreciate
freedom most.

Haruki Murakami

An artist's only

concern is to shoot

for some kind of

perfection, and on

his own terms, not

anyone else's.

J.D. Salinger

Nothing contributes
so much to tranquilise the
mind as a steady purpose
— a point on which the
soul may fix its
intellectual eye.

Mary Shelley

Words empty as

the wind are best left

unsaid.

Homer

Time is the only critic

without ambition.

John Steinbeck

Never hate your
enemies. It affects
your judgment.

Mario Puzo

Experience is the

only prophecy of

wise men.

Alphonse de Lamartine

Be vigilant, for

nothing one achieves

lasts forever.

Tahar Ben Jelloun

Our days and nights
have sorrows woven
with delights.

François de Malherbe

We tire of those pleasures
we take, but never of
those we give.

John Petit-Senn

Religions tend to

disappear with man's

good fortune.

Raymond Queneau

Even if happiness

forgets you a little bit,

never completely forget

about it.

Jacques Prevert

The dream, alone, is
of interest. What is life,
without a dream?

Edmond Rostand

We are enriched

by our reciprocate

differences.

Paul Valery

As I have not worried
to be born, I do not
worry to die.

Federico Garcia Lorca

Of what use is the
memory of facts, if not to
serve as an example of
good or of evil?

Alfred de Vigny

The test of good manners is to be patient with the bad ones.

Solomon Ibn Gabirol

Be content to be

what you are, and

prefer nothing to it,

and do not fear or wish

for your last day.

Marcus Valerius Martialis

Travellers,

there is no path;

paths are made

by walking.

Antonio Machado

Every day is

a journey, and

the journey itself is

home.

Matsuo Basho

Being entirely honest

with oneself

is a good exercise.

Sigmund Freud

There is no secret to

success

except hard work and

getting something

indefinable

which we call the breaks.

Countee Cullen

Labour is the
fabled magician's wand,
the philosopher's stone,
and the cap of
good fortune.

James Weldon Johnson

Love and death

are the two

great hinges

on which

all human sympathies

turn.

B.R. Hayden

If a man is

not faithful to his

own individuality,

he cannot be loyal

to anything.

Claude McKay

Loss is not felt

in the absence of

love.

Elizabeth Alexander

Stories can

conquer fear.

They can make

the heart

bigger.

Ben Okri

Let us keep

the dance of rain

our fathers kept

and tread our

dreams beneath

the jungle sky.

Arna Bontemps

It is not
our differences that
divide us.
It is our inability
to recognise,
accept, and
celebrate those
differences.

Audre Lorde

Cynicism is a form

of obedience.

Cornelius Eady

Find your

own voice and

use it.

Jayne Cortez

However stupid a
fool's words, they are
sometimes enough
to confound
an intelligent man.

Nikolai Gogol

Men can starve from
a lack of self-realisation
as much as they can
from a lack of bread.

Richard Wright

The end of
confession is
to tell the truth
to and for oneself.

J.M. Coetzee

If you want

to do anything,

do it now,

without compromise or

concession, because

you have only one life.

Gao Xingijan

People change

with time.

Günter Grass

It is not whether your

words or actions

are tough or gentle;

it is the spirit

behind your actions

and words

that announces your

inner state.

Rene Char

A person often meets

his destiny on the road

he took to avoid it.

Jean de La Fontaine

We consume
our tomorrows
fretting about our
yesterdays.

Persius

What is called

a sincere work is

one that is

endowed with

enough strength

to give reality

to an illusion.

Max Jacob

Friendship is also about liking a person for their failings, their weakness. It's also about mutual help, not about exploitation.

Paul Theroux

To be successful
in life what you need
is education, not
literacy and degrees.

Munshi Premchand

There's a way to

be good again.

Khaled Hosseini

It is the mark of
an educated
mind to be able
to entertain a
thought without
accepting it.

Aristotle

‘

A man whose life has

been dishonourable

is not entitled to

escape disgrace

in death.

Lucius Accius

No human trait

deserves less

tolerance

in everyday life,

and gets less, than

intolerance.

Giacomo Leopardi

You can't have
relationships with other
people until you give
birth to yourself.

Sonia Sanchez

True love cannot be
found where it does
not exist, nor can it be
denied where it does.

Torquato Tasso

A good laugh is

sunshine in the house.

William Makepeace Thackeray

The world is
a severe schoolmaster,
for its frowns are less
dangerous than its smiles
and flatteries, and
it is a difficult task
to keep in the path
of wisdom.

Phillis Wheatley

A man is either free
or he is not.
There cannot be any
apprenticeship for
freedom.

Amiri Baraka

Unexpected intrusions
of beauty. This is what
life is.

Saul Bellow

There must be

more to life than

having everything.

Maurice Sendak

Equality and
self-determination
should never be
divided in the
name of religious or
ideological fervour.

Rita Dove

Memories are like

mulligatawny soup

in a cheap restaurant.

It is best not to stir them.

P.G. Wodehouse

Ever tried. Ever failed. No

matter. Try Again.

Fail again.

Fail better.

Samuel Beckett

What happens

in the heart

simply happens.

Ted Hughes

To copy the truth

can be a good thing,

but to invent the truth

is better, much better.

Giuseppe Verdi

Make a difference

about something

other than

yourselves.

Toni Morrison

Complacency is

a state of mind

that exists only in

retrospective:

it has to be shattered

before being

ascertained.

Vladimir Nabokov

If you're walking down
the right path and
you're willing to keep
walking, eventually
you'll make progress.

Barack Obama

The thing about
inspiration is that
it takes your mind off
everything else.

Vikram Seth

The world is always

in movement.

V.S. Naipaul

One's life has value

so long as one

attributes value to

the life of others,

by means of love,

friendship, indignation

and compassion.

Simone de Beauvoir

If you shut up truth,

and bury it

underground,

it will but grow.

Émile Zola

Knowledge comes,

but wisdom lingers.

Alfred, Lord Tennyson

What matters most

is how well you walk

through the fire.

Charles Bukowski

The future is

no more uncertain

than the present.

Walt Whitman

It takes courage to

grow up and become

who you really are.

E.E. Cummings

There are no

strangers here;

only friends you

haven't yet met.

William Butler Yeats

Authority without
wisdom is like
a heavy axe
without
an edge,
fitter to bruise
than polish.

Anne Bradstreet

A classic is a book
that has never
finished saying
what it has to say.

Italo Calvino

All that counts in life

is intention.

Andrea Bocelli

Memory is the way we
keep telling ourselves
our stories — and
telling other people
a somewhat different
version of our stories.

Alice Munro

There is an
incompatibility between
literary creation and
political activity.

Mario Vargas Llosa

In the end,

we are all determined by

the place and the time

in which we were born.

Patrick Modiano

Conventionality is not morality.

Charlotte Bronte

Fortune favours the bold.

Virgil

Let your dreams

outgrow the shoes of

your expectations.

Ryunosuke Satoro

Don't confuse honours

with achievement.

Zadie Smith

If we wait for the moment
when everything,
absolutely everything is
ready, we shall
never begin.

Ivan Turgenev

Never mistake motion for
action.

Ernest Hemingway

In human relationships,
kindness and lies are
worth a thousand truths.

Graham Greene

Know how to live the time

that is given to you.

Dario Fo

The past is what

you remember,

imagine you remember,

convince yourself

you remember, or

pretend you remember.

Harold Pinter

Life is short, and

we should respect

every moment of it.

Orhan Pamuk